SINventory

A Sin Prayer Guide
for the Believer

Bruce A. Kugler

Publisher's Cataloging-in-Publication data

Names: Kugler, Bruce A., author.
Title: Sinventory: a sin prayer guide for the believer / Bruce A.
Kugler.
Description: Sherman, IL: Bruce A. Kugler, 2023.
Identifiers: LCCN: 2023910804 | ISBN: 979-8-9876214-2-4
(paperback) | 979-8-9876214-3-1 (ebook)
Subjects: LCSH Devotional calendars. | Prayer. | Sin--
Christianity. | BISAC RELIGION / Christian Living / Prayer |
RELIGION / Christian Living / Devotional | BODY, MIND &
SPIRIT / Healing / Prayer & Spiritual
Classification: LCC BT715 .K84 2023 | DDC 233.2--dc23

FORWARD

Revival! Thousands of revival meetings are held every year in the United States. However, only a very few churches experience true revival. Unfortunately, revival services are often only a series of poorly attended meetings.

God desires to bring revival to the church. Yet, believers are often not willing to receive revival on God's terms. Revival only comes when believers, in response to the conviction of the Holy Spirit, humble themselves and turn to God through repentance of sin. Without genuine repentance there will be no revival. Repentance prepares the heart for the fullness of the Holy Spirit and the movement of God in a church. Unrepented sin is what prevents revival in many churches.

The Sinventory is a prayer guide for the believer. A person who has not experienced salvation will not find peace with God by merely refraining from certain sins or attempting to live a holy life. It is only by receiving forgiveness of sin through the death, burial, and resurrection of Jesus Christ that a person inherits eternal life. Furthermore, a person who has received Jesus Christ as his Lord and Savior never needs to fear the wrath of God because the penalty of his sin has been paid by Jesus Christ through the shedding of His blood on the cross.

After salvation, the Holy Spirit will convict the believer when he or she sins. If the believer ignores the conviction of the Holy Spirit and fails to repent, sin will begin to gain power over the believer. The believer has an eternal relationship with God that can never be severed. However, sin can block the believer's fellowship with God. Satan can also use unrepented sin to obtain a foothold in the believer's life to create a spiritual bondage.

Often the believer does not take enough time from his busy schedule to read and meditate on the Word of God and allow the Holy Spirit to point out sin in his life. At other times, the Holy Spirit will convict the believer of sin, but he or she fails to promptly repent and soon forgets that they sinned against God.

The Sinventory quotes key portions of Scripture and provides questions for the believer to consider and reflect upon. During this process, the Holy Spirit will point out unrepented sins in the believer's life. These sins may be hindering the believer from experiencing personal revival and growing spiritually. However, the Sinventory should not be used as a legalistic guide to find sin. The believer should only repent of sin based on the conviction of the Holy Spirit.

<u>Example prayer for God to reveal unrepented sin</u>:

"Heavenly Father, I pray that You would put Your searchlight on my heart and bring to my mind sins that I have committed in the past but have never repented from. I want to make sure that all doors in my life that I have opened to the powers of darkness are closed."

<u>Example prayer to repent of sin</u>:

"Heavenly Father, I repent of _____. I turn from this sin. I thank you for the forgiveness that I have because Jesus Christ shed His blood on the cross. Please cleanse me from this sin. I now shut the door in my life to the powers

of darkness that I previously opened by this un-repented sin."

"If we confess our sins, He is faithful and righteous to forgive us our sins and to cleanse us from all unrighteousness" (1 John 1:9).

LYING

"Do not lie to one another, since you laid aside the old self with its evil practices" (Col. 3:9).

Have you lied? Have you been untruthful by withholding information or twisting the truth? Have you lied at your job? Have you lied to your spouse? Have you lied on your income taxes? Have you slandered someone? Have you listened to someone slander another person when you could have avoided the situation?

COMPLAINING

"Do all things without grumbling or disputing" (Phil. 2:14).

Have you grumbled or complained? Have you complained to God? Have you complained about the way God made you? Have you complained to God that He has not given you the money you think you need? Have you complained about your church? Have you grumbled about the working conditions at your job or not having a job? Have you nagged and complained to your spouse? Have you complained to others about your spouse?

GOSSIP

"I am afraid that perhaps when I come I may find you to be not what I wish and may be found by you to

be not what you wish; that perhaps there will be strife, jealousy, angry tempers, disputes, slanders, gossip, arrogance, disturbances"
(2 Cor. 12:20).

Have you gossiped? Have you gossiped about your pastor? Have you gossiped about a co-worker or your boss? Have you said something that was true about another person but was not edifying or was said in anger, envy, or bitterness? Have you posted on social media unkind remarks about someone? Have you ever gossiped about celebrities, politicians, or people you do not know personally?

Selfishness

"Do nothing from selfishness or empty conceit, but with humility of mind regard one another as more

important than yourselves" (Phil. 2:3).

Have you been selfish? Have you been self-ish with your material possessions? Have you been selfish with your time? Have you been sexually selfish with your spouse?

LUST FOR POWER

"An argument started among them as to which of them might be the greatest. But Jesus, knowing what they were thinking in their heart, took a child and stood him by His side, and said to them, 'Whoever receives this child in My name receives Me, and whoever receives Me receives Him who sent Me; for the one who is least among all of you, this is the one who is great'" (Luke 9:46-48).

Have you desired to be great in the world's eyes? Have you lusted for power over people? Do you fantasize about being a man or woman of great wealth? Is it your ambition to be a famous evangelist, pastor, or minister regardless of God's will for your life? Have you fantasized about being a great businessman, rock star, actor, politician, or world leader and having people idolize you?

STUBBORNNESS

"Because of your stubbornness and unrepentant heart you are storing up wrath for yourself in the day of wrath and revelation of the righteous judgment of God" (Rom. 2:5).

Have you been stubborn? Have you been stubborn in accepting other people's advice? Have you been stubborn with your spouse in refusing to listen to her or his suggestions? Do you always want to be the decision maker? Do you have to have your way in the church as a condition of your support and cooperation? Have you been stubborn in not obeying God?

IMPATIENCE

"We urge you, brethren, admonish the unruly, encourage the faint-hearted, help the weak, be patient with everyone" (1 Thess. 5:14).

Have you been impatient with people? Have you been impatient with your spouse or children? Have you been impatient with your co-workers? Have you been impatient with yourself? Have you been impatient with God?

ARGUMENTS

"The Lord's bond-servant must not be quarrelsome, but be kind to all, able to teach, patient when wronged" *(2 Tim. 2:24).*

Have you been argumentative or quarrelsome? Have you quarreled or bickered with your spouse, parents, or children? Do you provoke quarrels by making abrasive comments? Have you argued about Bible doctrine? Have you ever been argumentative at a church business meeting?

TEMPER

"A fool always loses his temper, But a wise man holds it back" *(Prov. 29:11).*

Have you lost your temper? Have you lost your temper with your spouse or children? Have you lost your temper while at your job, school, church, or a social setting? Have you lost your temper with a stranger, i.e., over the phone, when you feel you are not getting the response you desire?

BITTERNESS

"Let all bitterness and wrath and anger and clamor and slander be put away from you, along with all malice" (Eph. 4:31).

Have you been bitter toward anyone? Have you been bitter at God? Have you been bitter against a former employer? Have you been bitter at your spouse? Are you bitter because you believe someone has let you down by not meeting your expectations?

Unforgiveness

"If you forgive others for their transgressions, your heavenly Father will also forgive you. But if you do not forgive others, then your Father will not forgive your transgressions" (Matt. 6:14-15).

Is there anyone that you continue to hold a grudge against? Is there anyone, including a business partner, ex-spouse, pastor, or relative, who has hurt you in the past that you have not forgiven? Have you forgiven yourself of sins you have sincerely repented of?

Revenge

"Never take your own revenge, beloved, but leave room for the wrath of God, for it is written, 'Vengeance

is Mine, I will repay,' says the Lord. But if your enemy is hungry, feed him, and if he is thirsty, give him a drink; for in so doing you will heap burning coals upon his head'" (Rom. 12:19-20).

Have you taken revenge against someone? Do you have vengeful thoughts in your heart? Do you wish you could kill or harm someone? Do you have thoughts of destroying someone financially or destroying someone's business? Do you think about getting even with people who have wronged you in the past?

HATE

"We also once were foolish ourselves, disobedient, deceived, enslaved to various lusts and pleasures, spending our life in malice

and envy, hateful, hating one another" (Titus 3:3).

Have you hated anyone? Do you hate your boss or teachers? Do you hate your parents or in-laws? If you are divorced, do you hate your former spouse? Do you hate your government leaders?

PROFANITY

"Let no unwholesome word proceed from your mouth, but only such a word is good for edification according to the need of the moment, so that it may give grace to those who hear" (Eph. 4:29).

Have you used unwholesome language? Do you swear? Have you used words to verbal

ly abuse or demean another person? Have
you used God's name in vain?

IMMORAL JOKES

*"There must be no filthiness and
silly talk, or coarse jesting, which
are not fitting, but rather giving of
thanks" (Eph. 5:4).*

Have you told filthy or immoral jokes? Have
you listened to an immoral joke when you
could have avoided the situation?

STEALING

"You shall not steal" (Exod. 20:15).

Have you stolen anything? Have you shop-
lifted? Have you stolen anything from your
employer? Have you exaggerated income

tax deductions? Have you claimed business deductions for things that were not business related? Have you engaged in personal activities on your employer's time? Have you used your employer's equipment or supplies for personal matters without permission?

DOUBT

"He must ask in faith without any doubting, for the one who doubts is like the surf of the sea, driven and tossed by the wind" (Jam. 1:6).

Have you doubted the Word of God? Do you doubt that God loves you? Do you doubt that God exists? Do you doubt that God is all powerful? Do you doubt that God can provide your physical needs? Do you doubt that God can work for His glory in the difficult circumstances of your life?

UNBELIEF

"You will say then, 'Branches were broken off so that I might be grafted in.' Quite right, they were broken off for their unbelief, but you stand by your faith. Do not be conceited, but fear; for if God did not spare the natural branches, He will not spare you, either" (Rom. 11:19-21).

Have you chosen to not believe certain portions of the Word of God? Have you rationalized certain passages of Scripture to justify a moral failure in your life?

LACK OF THANKSGIVING

"Devote yourselves to prayer, keeping alert in it with an attitude of thanksgiving" (Col. 4:2).

Have you failed to maintain an attitude of praise and thanksgiving? Have you failed to thank God for the good things that He has brought into your life? Do you give thanks in all things even for the difficult circumstances in your life? Have you neglected personal praise and worship?

LACK OF PRAYER

"Pray without ceasing" (1 Thess. 5:17).

Have you neglected prayer? Have you failed to make prayer a priority in your life? Have you made significant decisions in your life without consulting God?

INEFFECTIVE PRAYER

"When you are praying, do not use meaningless repetition, as the Gentiles do, for they suppose that they will be heard for their many words" (Matt. 6:7).

Do you pray out of a sense of obligation rather than a desire to develop a personal relationship with God? Have you used meaningless repetition when addressing God? If you pray before your meals, has it become a mere habit? Do you pray about material things when you know there is unrepented sin in your life?

LACK OF BIBLE STUDY

"Be diligent to present yourself approved to God as a workman who does not need to be ashamed, accu-

rately handling the word of truth"
(2 Tim. 2:15).

Have you neglected to read and study the Bible? Do you feel you know everything about the Bible? Do you have an unteachable heart? Are you seeking God's guidance when you read God's Word?

LACK OF FELLOWSHIP

"Not forsaking our own assembling together, as is the habit of some, but encouraging one another, and all the more, as you see the day drawing near" (Heb. 10:25).

Have you neglected fellowship with other believers? Do you feel you do not need fellowship with other believers to grow spiritually? Have you failed to fellowship with others to meet their spiritual needs? Have you excused yourself from attending a local church because you have not found the "perfect church" or believe that you do not need "organized religion?"

RELATIONSHIP TO GOD

"Behold, I stand at the door and knock; if anyone hears My voice and opens the door, I will come into him, and will dine with him, and he with Me" (Rev. 3:20).

Have you substituted going to church for a personal relationship with God? Have you confused religious busyness with personally knowing God? Do you find yourself going through religious motions without your heart really being involved?

TITHES AND OFFERINGS

*"Woe to you, scribes and Phari-
sees, hypocrites! For you tithe mint
and dill and cummin, and have
neglected the weightier provisions
of the law: justice and mercy and
faithfulness; but these are the things
you should have done without ne-
glecting the others" (Matt. 23:23).*

Have you neglected to give of your financial
resources to God's work? Have you ever
prayed and sincerely asked God to show
you how much you should give to your
church and to other ministries? Have you
ever given an offering grudgingly? Have
you ever given with selfish motives?

GREED

"Immorality or any impurity or greed must not even be named among you, as is proper among saints" (Eph. 5:3).

Have you been greedy? Have you failed to meet the physical needs of others? Do you resent churches or charities asking for donations? Have you hoarded money? Have you put your faith in your savings account or investments rather than trusting God for your future needs?

LACK OF DISCIPLINE

"Even though I am absent in body, nevertheless I am with you in spirit, rejoicing to see your good discipline and the stability of your faith in Christ" (Col. 2:5).

Do you lack discipline in spending money? Have you purchased items you could not afford? Have you lacked discipline in physical exercise? Have you failed to treat your body as the temple of the Holy Spirit? Do your habits harm your body? Have you failed to give your body the rest it needs?

EATING HABITS

"Many walk, of whom I often told you, and now tell you even weeping, that they are enemies of the cross of Christ, whose end is destruction, whose god is their appetite, and whose glory is in their shame, who set their minds on earthly things" (Phil. 3:18-19).

Is your god your appetite? Do you overeat when you are depressed or discouraged? Have you listened to the Holy Spirit in deciding the types and amounts of food you should eat? Are you overweight or under-weight because of poor eating habits?

ALCOHOL

"Do you not know that the unrigh-teous shall not inherit the king-dom of God? Do not be deceived; neither fornicators, nor idolaters, nor adulterers, nor effeminate, nor homosexuals, nor thieves, nor the covetous, nor drunkards, nor revil-ers, nor swindlers, will inherit the kingdom of God" (1 Cor. 6:9-10).

Have you been drunk? Do you drink alcohol when you are depressed or discour-aged? Are you dependent on alcohol to get through the day? Do you drink alcohol instead of turning to God to ease your emotional hurts?

LAZINESS

"Laziness casts into a deep sleep, and an idle man will suffer hunger" (Prov. 19:15).

Have you been lazy? Have you been lazy at your job? Have you been lazy about Bible study? Have you been lazy about cleaning and taking care of your home? Have you been lazy about providing for the physical needs of your family?

JEALOUSY

"You are still fleshly. For since there is jealousy and strife among you, are you not fleshly, and are

you not walking like mere men?"
(1 Cor. 3:3).

Have you been jealous? Have you been jealous of someone because of her or his appearance, possessions, finances, talents, or vocation? Have you been jealous of another person's spiritual gift? Are you jealous of the ministry of a famous minister or evangelist? Pastors, are you jealous because of the large attendance at another church or the size of the church building?

Covetousness

"You shall not covet your neighbor's house; you shall not covet your neighbor's wife or his male servant or his female servant or his ox or his donkey or anything that belongs to your neighbor" (Exod. 20:17).

Have you coveted someone's home, car, family, or lifestyle? Have you coveted the income someone else earns? Have you coveted material possessions? Do you wish you were married to someone else?

PRIDE

"When pride comes, then comes dishonor, But with the humble is wisdom" (Prov. 11:2).

Have you been prideful? Are you prideful of your education, occupation, or position in the church? Have you given God the glory for your accomplishments? Do you believe you are self-sufficient and really do not need any help from God? Are you prideful of your appearance? Are you proud that you give more money to the church than other people?

BRAGGING

"Love is patient, love is kind and is not jealous; love does not brag and is not arrogant" (1 Cor. 13:4).

Have you bragged? Have you bragged about how much of the Bible you know? Have you bragged about the material possessions you own? Do you always talk about yourself and your accomplishments?

DEPRESSION

"We know that God causes all things to work together for good to those who love God, to those who are called according to His purpose" (Rom. 8:28).

Have you doubted that God can use your mistakes and the trials in your life for good? Have you given into attitudes of despair or depression? Is your life easily crushed by your circumstances because you have failed to trust in the Word of God?

LONELINESS

"I am convinced that neither death, nor life, nor angels, nor principalities, nor things present, nor things to come, nor powers, nor height, nor depth, nor any other created thing, will be able to separate us from the love of God, which is in Christ Jesus our Lord" (Rom. 8:38-39).

Have you allowed loneliness to control your life instead of claiming the presence of Christ? Have you tried to fill a void in your life with human relationships as a substitute for a deep relationship with God?

REJECTION

"If anyone is in Christ, he is a new creature; the old things passed away; behold, new things have come" (2 Cor. 5:17).

Have you dwelt on thoughts of self-rejection? Have you believed the lie that you are worthless? Have you dwelt on thoughts of self-pity?

INFERIORITY

"Blessed be the God and Father of our Lord Jesus Christ, who has blessed us with every spiritual blessing in the heavenly places in

Christ, just as He chose us in Him
before the foundation of the world,
that we would be holy and blame-
less before Him" (Eph. 1:3-4).

Have you dwelt on thoughts of inferiority?
Have you failed to believe how valuable you
are to God? Have you been more concerned
about what people think of you rather than
what Jesus Christ thinks of you? Have you
been overly self-conscious?

MURDER

"Everyone who hates his brother is
a murderer; and you know that no
murderer has eternal life abiding in
him" (1 John 3:15).

Have you ever murdered anyone? Do you
fantasize about murdering someone? Have

you ever wished someone was dead? Have you ever attempted suicide? Have you dwelt on thoughts of suicide?

ABORTION

"There are six things which the Lord hates, Yes, seven which are an abomination to Him: Haughty eyes, a lying tongue, And hands that shed innocent blood" (Prov. 6:16-17).

Have you ever had an abortion? Have you ever encouraged or assisted someone in having an abortion?

PREJUDICE

"He [Jesus] also told this parable to some people who trusted in themselves that they were righteous, and

viewed others with contempt: 'Two men went up into the temple to pray, one a Pharisee and the other a tax collector. The Pharisee stood and was praying this to himself, God, I thank You that I am not like other people: swindlers, unjust, adulterers, or even like this tax collector'" (Luke 18:9-11).

Have you ever been prejudiced toward people of a different race? Have you looked down at others who are different than you? Have you been prejudiced against those who are overweight? Have you shown hatred or been violent towards homosexuals? Have you been prejudiced toward people who have more or less money than you? Do you judge people who dress differently, have longer or shorter hair than you, or have tattoos?

Harmful Music

"Let the word of Christ richly dwell within you, with all wisdom teaching and admonishing one another with psalms and hymns and spiritual songs, singing with thankfulness in your hearts to God" *(Col. 3:16).*

Have you willfully listened to music which had immoral lyrics? Have you idolized a musician who you knew was on drugs or had an immoral lifestyle?

Sexual Immorality

"Flee immorality. Every other sin that a man commits is outside the body, but the immoral man sins against his own body" *(1 Cor. 6:18).*

Have you committed sexual sin? Have you entertained sexual fantasies? Have you looked at pornography? Have you seen a movie or video that had an immoral sexual scene?

ADULTERY

"Marriage is to be held in honor among all, and the marriage bed is to be undefiled; for fornicators and adulterers God will judge" (Heb. 13:4).

Have you ever committed adultery? Have you ever committed fornication? Have you fantasized about having sex with someone other than your spouse?

INCEST

"If there is a man who lies with his daughter in-law, both of them shall surely be put to death; they have committed incest, their bloodguiltiness is upon them" (Lev. 20:12).

Have you committed incest? Have you dwelt on thoughts of committing incest? Have you ever sexually abused a child?

HOMOSEXUALITY

"For this reason God gave them over to degrading passions; for their women exchanged the natural function for that which is unnatural, and in the same way also the men abandoned the natural function of the woman and burned in their desire toward one another, men with

men committing indecent acts and receiving in their own persons the due penalty of their error" (Rom. 1:26-27).

Have you allowed thoughts of homosexual or lesbian behavior to linger in your mind? Have you yielded to thoughts of same sex attraction? Have you ever engaged in homosexual or lesbian acts?

GUILT

"There is now no condemnation for those who are in Christ Jesus" (Rom. 8:1).

Have you condemned yourself for your past sins? Have you failed to believe that God is willing to forgive you of every sin you have ever committed? Do you condemn yourself because you think that you have failed others? Have you submitted to thoughts of guilt because you think that you have failed as a parent?

FEAR

"There is no fear in love; but perfect love casts out fear, because fear involves punishment, and the one who fears is not perfected in love" (1 John 4:18).

Have you allowed your mind to dwell on thoughts of irrational fears? Do you have a fear of death or a fear of sickness? Are you afraid of Satan or demons? Are you afraid of the dark or heights?

WORRY

"Be anxious for nothing, but in ev-
erything by prayer and supplication
with thanksgiving let your requests
be made known to God" (Phil. 4:6).

Do you worry? Do you rationalize your worry by calling it merely concern? Have you worried about what other people think of you? Do you worry that you may get sick? Do you worry about your children or your parents? Have you worried about finances? Do you worry about losing your job or being laid off? Have you failed to believe that it is God who provides your physical and material needs?

REBELLION

"Rebellion is as the sin of divina-
tion, And insubordination is as

iniquity and idolatry. Because you have rejected the word of the Lord, He has also rejected you from being king" (1 Sam. 15:23).

Have you been rebellious? Have you rebelled against your parents? Have you rebelled against school authority, police, or other civic authority? Do you have a rebellious attitude toward your pastor or other spiritual leaders in the church? Are you rebelling against what you know God wants you to do or stop doing?

HUSBANDS AND WIVES

"As the church is subject to Christ, so also the wives ought to be to their husbands in everything. Husbands, love your wives, just as Christ also loved the church and gave Himself up for her" (Eph. 5:24-25).

Husbands, have you failed to love your wife as Jesus Christ loves the church? Have you failed to make sacrifices for your wife? Wives, have you failed to be submissive to your husbands in everything that is not directly contrary to the Word of God? Do you treat your spouse as if he or she has no value or worth? Have you tried to control your spouse? Have you hidden financial information from your spouse?

Drugs

"I urge you, brethren, by the mercies of God, to present your bodies a living and holy sacrifice, acceptable to God, which is your spiritual service of worship. And do not be conformed to this world, but be transformed by the renewing of your mind, that you may prove what the will of God is, that which is good

and acceptable and perfect" (Rom. 12:1-2).

Have you ever used illegal drugs? Have you abused prescription drugs? Have you used mind altering drugs for recreational purposes even if they are legal?

WITCHCRAFT

"There shall not be found among you anyone who makes his son or his daughter pass through the fire, one who uses divination, one who practices witchcraft, or one who interprets omens, or a sorcerer, or one who casts a spell, or a medium, or a spiritist, or one who calls up the dead" (Deut. 18:10-11).

Have you ever been involved with witch-craft, Satanism, fortune telling, or astral projection? Have you ever been involved in visualization or palm reading? Have you ever tried to develop ESP or Ki? Have you ever participated in an animal or human sacrifice?

ASTROLOGY

"You are wearied with your many counsels; Let now the astrologers, Those who prophesy by the stars, Those who predict by the new moons, Stand up and save you from what will come upon you" (Isa. 47:13).

Have you ever been involved with astrology? Have you ever read your horoscope, even just for fun?

CHANNELING

"When they say to you, 'Consult the mediums and the spiritists who whisper and mutter,' should not a people consult their God? Should they consult the dead on behalf of the living?" (Isa. 8:19).

Have you ever consulted a psychic or a medium? Have you ever participated in a seance? Have you ever played with a ouija board? Have you ever asked for guidance from any spirit other than the Holy Spirit?

OCCULT OBJECTS

"Many of those who practiced magic brought their books together and began burning them in the sight of everyone; and they counted up the

price of them and found it fifty thou-
sand pieces of silver" (Acts 19:19).

Have you ever read or possessed occult books? Have you ever possessed occult objects or jewelry? Have you ever possessed a ouija board, tarot cards, or a crystal ball?

FALSE RELIGION

"I am afraid that, as the serpent deceived Eve by his craftiness, your minds will be led astray from the simplicity and purity of devotion to Christ. For if one comes and preaches another Jesus whom we have not preached, or you receive a different spirit which you have not received, or a different gospel which you have not accepted, you bear this beautifully" (2 Cor. 11:3-4).

Have you ever been involved with Buddhism, Hinduism, Jehovah's Witnesses, Mormonism, New Age, or any other false religion or philosophy?

VIOLENCE

"The Lord tests the righteous and the wicked, And the one who loves violence His soul hates" (Ps. 11:5).

Have you dwelt on thoughts of violence? Have you watched movies or videos for entertainment that had violent scenes? Have you ever been involved in karate or other martial arts where meditation was taught? Have you ever visualized punching, kicking, killing, or sexually attacking someone?

INTERNET AND MEDIA

"Whether, then, you eat or drink or whatever you do, do all to the glory of God" (1 Cor. 10:31).

Have you wasted time with television, videos, movies, internet, and social media? Is your time with God cut short because you prefer time on the internet? Do you view material that does not glorify God?

PRACTICAL SUGGESTIONS

Allowing the Holy Spirit to take an inventory of your life can take an extraordinary amount of time. It is not unusual to be convicted by the Holy Spirit of dozens of sins in any particular sin category. Thus, it is improbable that a person could pray through the Sinventory in one evening. It could take weeks or even months to complete. Furthermore, it is not sufficient to merely read the Sinventory if you truly desire to experience personal revival. Instead, after each verse and comment is read, the believer should ask God to reveal any sin that exists in his or her life. Without prayer and the leadership of the Holy Spirit, the believer will become overly introspective, which can lead to self-condemnation.

Believers can become discouraged when their lives are compared to the absolute standard of the Word of God. However, the believer only deceives himself when he justifies unrepented sin. It is this sin that often hinders the believer from experiencing love, joy, and peace. Although sin sometimes brings temporary pleasure, it always brings eventual sorrow. Believers must submit their life to the authority of the Word of God and be honest with themselves if they desire to have intimate fellowship with God and experience personal revival.

Finally, the believer should never condemn himself regardless of the type or amount of sin that has been committed. Jesus Christ has paid the penalty for the believer's sin. This is why the Apostle Paul stated, "There is now no condemnation for those who are in Christ Jesus" (Rom. 8:1). God no longer condemns the believer for his sin; therefore, neither should the believer condemn himself. The Holy Spirit convicts the believer of sin to allow him the opportunity to repent so the sin that is hindering the fullness and blessing of God can be removed. The wonderful truth revealed in the Bible is God has promised that He is willing to extend His grace to the believer no matter how great the sin or the number of sins in their life.

Special thanks are given to the following individuals who provided comments and suggestions on the content of the Sinventory:

Pastor John Somers
Pastor Randy Newton
Pastor Steve Hardin
Pastor Andy Gillespie
Marjorie Kugler

www.ingramcontent.com/pod-product-compliance
Lightning Source LLC
Chambersburg PA
CBHW060355130626
46553CB00003B/1244